Elvis Presley

T0082991

CONTENTS

HOW TO USE THE CD ACCOMPANIMENT:

THE CD IS PLAYABLE ON ANY CD PLAYER, AND IS ALSO ENHANCED SO MAC AND PC USERS CAN ADJUST THE RECORDING TO ANY TEMPO WITHOUT CHANGING THE PITCH.

A MELODY CUE APPEARS ON THE RIGHT CHANNEL ONLY. IF YOUR CD PLAYER HAS A BALANCE ADJUSTMENT, YOU CAN ADJUST THE VOLUME OF THE MELODY BY TURNING DOWN THE RIGHT CHANNEL.

ISBN 978-1-4234-6696-3

HAL•LEONARD®
CORPORATION
7777 W. BLUEMOUND RD. P.O. BOX 13819 MILWAUKEE, WI 53213

Visit Hal Leonard Online at
www.halleonard.com

◆ ALL SHOOK UP

Horn

Words and Music by OTIS BLACKWELL
and ELVIS PRESLEY

② BLUE SUEDE SHOES

Words and Music by
CARL LEE PERKINS

Horn

❖ ③ CAN'T HELP FALLING IN LOVE

Horn

Words and Music by GEORGE DAVID WEISS,
HUGO PERETTI and LUIGI CREATORE

◆ 4 DON'T BE CRUEL
(To a Heart That's True)

Horn

Words and Music by OTIS BLACKWELL
and ELVIS PRESLEY

Rock 'n' Roll Shuffle

◆ HOUND DOG

Horn

Words and Music by JERRY LEIBER
and MIKE STOLLER

I WANT YOU, I NEED YOU, I LOVE YOU

HORN

Words and Music by MAURICE MYSELS
and IRA KOSLOFF

❼ IT'S NOW OR NEVER

Horn

Words and Music by AARON SCHROEDER
and WALLY GOLD

8 JAILHOUSE ROCK

HORN

Words and Music by JERRY LEIBER
and MIKE STOLLER

Rock 'n' Roll

◆ 9 LOVE ME

HORN

Words and Music by JERRY LEIBER
and MIKE STOLLER

⬥❿ LOVE ME TENDER

Horn

Words and Music by ELVIS PRESLEY
and VERA MATSON

⑪ LOVING YOU

HORN

Words and Music by JERRY LEIBER
and MIKE STOLLER

⟨12⟩ RETURN TO SENDER

Horn

Words and Music by OTIS BLACKWELL
and WINFIELD SCOTT

◆13 (LET ME BE YOUR) TEDDY BEAR

HORN

Words and Music by KAL MANN
and BERNIE LOWE

◆ TOO MUCH

Horn

Words and Music by LEE ROSENBERG
and BERNARD WEINMAN

◆15 WEAR MY RING AROUND YOUR NECK

Horn

Words and Music by BERT CARROLL
and RUSSELL MOODY